Collector's Guide T

SNOW DOMES

IDENTIFICATION & VALUES

Helene Guarnaccia

Many thanks to Herb Rabbin who created this dome.

COLLECTOR BOOKS
A Division of Schroeder Publishing Co., Inc.

The current values in this book should be used only as a guide. They are not intended to set prices, which vary from one section of the country to another. Auction prices as well as dealer prices vary greatly and are affected by condition as well as demand. Neither the Author nor the Publisher assumes responsibility for any losses that might be incurred as a result of consulting this guide.

COVER PHOTOS — TOP: Dome is made of handblown glass, one of a kind; the base is also glass. It was executed by Canadian artist Wendy Allen and purchased at a craft show in Baltimore. $150.00 – 200.00. CENTER LEFT: Moon Landing, tall dome, all silver. $20.00 – 22.00. Moon Landing, small oval dome, German made. $8.00 – 10.00. CENTER RIGHT: Pisa. $35.00 – 45.00. BOTTOM LEFT: From left to right: London Bobby (2), The Beefeater, and the Palace Guard (2). $8.00 – 10.00 each. BOTTOM RIGHT: Snow White in glass globe atop house. Walt Disney Company. Music box plays "Some Day My Prince Will Come." $40.00 new.

Searching For A Publisher?

We are always looking for knowledgeable people considered to be experts within their fields. If you feel that there is a real need for a book on your collectible subject and have a large comprehensive collection, contact us.

COLLECTOR BOOKS
P.O. Box 3009
Paducah, Kentucky 42002-3009

Cover Design by Sherry Kraus
Book Design by Gina Lage
Copy Editing by Rose Volkholz

TABLE OF CONTENTS

ACKNOWLEDGMENTS

There are so many people to thank when one is putting together a project of this magnitude. I certainly could not have done this book without a lot of help from a lot of people.

First and foremost, I want to thank Steve Green, who made his entire collection of 3,000 domes available to me. Steve was of constant good cheer and had never ending patience. David Peters and I camped out at his house for four straight days, and Steve helped us clean, refill, and sort his vast collection of domes. He not only stayed calm throughout this intrusion, but fed us as well!

David and Jan Peters put me up and put up with me for six days while we worked on this book. David was the principal photographer for the project, and spent two full days shooting in natural light to reduce glare; every time the sun moved, so did all the equipment! (Being from New England, I was incredulous that in Los Angeles in August people could leave things outside for days and be sure it would not rain.)

Marcia Leong came down for a day from San Francisco to help, and to offer her expert knowledge. Andy Zito helped with pricing and contributed some great domes, as did Michael Muntner, from Bethesda, Maryland. Michael even did his own photography!

Locally, Roman Woloszyn photographed (indoors!) a wonderful collection of foreign domes loaned to me by Carol Hofflich, and Phil Blumenkrantz brought over some domes from his collection as well.

Paul Huber made available some original art work that he had done using snow domes. The snow dome for the Mirage Hotel, and the snow dome for the 1981 Loucks Atelier Christmas party were created by him.

Collectors are fun people, and everyone who helped, helped to make this a fun undertaking. I am most appreciative, and only hope that the end result will justify everyone's time and trouble!

Sorting the domes at Steve Green's in California.

4

INTRODUCTION

Writing a price guide is a two-edged sword: collectors worry that a "book" will make the prices go up; on the other hand, a book also tends to validate a collectible, and therefore makes a collection worth more.

Another factor, besides price, is availability. I have been to many flea markets and antique shows, and when I asked for snow domes, I've been told by dealers that they didn't know they were worth anything, and so didn't bring them to display. Once a book comes out, so do the snow domes!

I'm sure that Nancy McMichael's book *Snowdomes*, published by Abbeville Press, has already raised the consciousness of the collecting world. In fact it was when I first saw her collection that I wanted to do this book.

Snow domes are everywhere: new ones in airports and souvenir shops, old ones in antique shops and flea markets. They are called "snowstorms" in England, snow globes, and "shakies." But when asking for them by any name, I can never stop myself from a twist of the wrist as I describe what I'm looking for. My biggest disappointment was at an otherwise perfect recent trip to Disney World, the capital of kitsch and souvenirs — not one snow dome, other than Christmas, was available.

Older snow domes were made of glass. The bases were either black Bakelite, or in the case of the Atlas Glass Company the bases were ceramic. The newer glass globes have wooden bases and frequently incorporate music boxes.

For most collectors, however, the most desirable are the ones of specific places — especially remote and little heard of amusement parks or tourist attractions. Advertising domes are also desirable as they, too, are identifiable. Cartoon characters are another category considered highly collectible.

The earliest snow domes were paperweights from France made in the 1840s and 50s. In the twentieth century many globes were made in Germany and Japan. In the 1950s plastic took over the market; these were manufactured in Hong Kong, and others in West Germany and Austria. Wherever they're from, and whatever they depict, the world inside a snow dome is a world of fantasy, beloved by children and adults alike. So enjoy your acquisitions, your treasures, and most of all, enjoy the hunt!

SNOW DOMES IN PRINT

The proliferation of snow domes in the media attests, I think, to their increasing collectibilty and popularity. There have been innumerable advertisements and cartoons using snow domes. I have not been able to get permission to reprint some of them. However, here are just a few of the many I have seen since I started work on this book.

San Francisco snow dome — a photograph of the Golden Gate Bridge. Christmas Card by ©Palm Press, Inc., 1442A Walnut Street #120, Berkeley, California 94709.

Snow dome for ad for the Mirage Hotel in Las Vegas. This dome was assembled by Paul Huber, of Hal Riney & Partners of San Francisco. The dome is a composite of three different city skylines to create a generic dome.

The Cambridge Center for Adult Education. Cover illustration by Katherine Mahoney of Belmont, Massachusetts. Art director: Deborah Chandler.

Advertisement for Lord & Taylor Christmas catalogue, 1992. The illustration was done by Joyce Patti, represented by Vicki Morgan Associates, New York City.

Shoebox Greetings
(a tiny little division of Hallmark)

Christmas trees with one tree in globe. Illustrated by Dick Daniels.

Card with four scenes. Illustrated by Payton Kelly.

Card with three frames of snowmen (and women) in domes. Illustrated by Becky Wilson Kelly.

Card with a weather forecast — "Life in a Snow Globe!" Illustrated by Eric Brace.

Christmas card: snowman in globe. Illustrated by Steven Guarnaccia for the Museum of Modern Art, New York.

Happy Holi-Daze card by David Peters, a California illustrator.

A New Year's card by and of David Peters with his wife, Jan.

*Come Celebrate
the 1981 Loucks Atelier
"Moved and Not Quite Settled/
Merry Christmas Party".*

*Thursday, December 17, 4-7 pm.
2900 Weslayan, Suite 530
Houston, Texas
R.S.V.P. 713-877-8551*

Be there. Aloha.

Card for Christmas party for Loucks Atelier, 1981. Dome hand built by Paul Huber of Hal Riney & Partners.

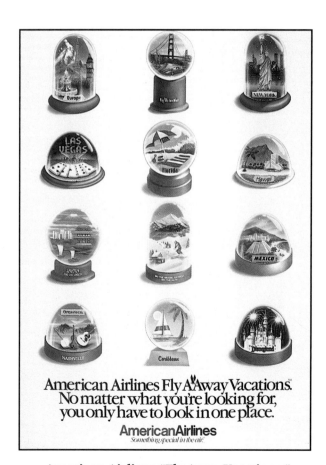

American Airlines "Fly Away Vacations."

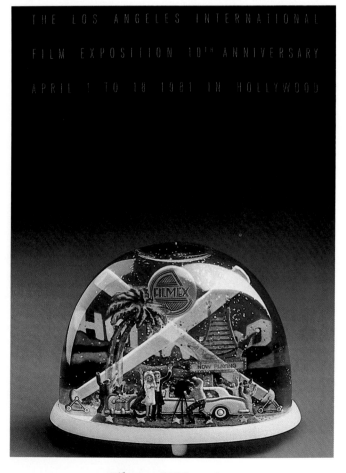

Filmex, 1981 poster.

Cover illustration by Kathy Osborn Young; © 1990 The New Yorker Magazine, Inc. Reprinted by Special Permission. All Rights Reserved.

ADVERTISING

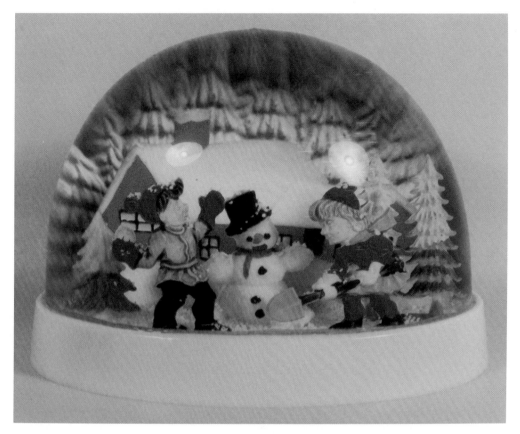

ANATOMY OF A SNOW DOME COMMERCIAL

By Paige Wilson

When people at The Disney Channel decided they wanted to use a snow dome as the centerpiece of a commercial to promote their cable network during the holiday season, they set about trying to find a dome that matched their ideal, but they couldn't find one. Several domes contained one usable element each — the right kids, the right shape, the right snow, the right house — but none was just right.

With the help of Steve Green in Los Angeles (owner of the various domes that they liked) the production company working on the ad linked up with Herb Rabbin, who had done "plastic surgery" before to repair broken domes and create a few of his own. The thought was that Herb could build a custom-made dome for Disney from the salvaged parts of Steve's domes.

Days followed, full of "snow tests," resolution of the glitter questions, seeing if the dome parts would recombine intact, unscratched, unclouded — all with shooting of the commercial fast approaching. The dome had to be flawless, for it would be the full-frame focus of the ad, with just a "hand model's" hand lifting it, shaking it, and putting it down again.

Fortunately, the dome came together beautifully and looks really authentic. To be on the safe side, the ad company asked Herb to be on hand at the shooting of the commercial on October 20, 1992, and it should run on non-cable television stations through November and December of this year [1992]. When you see it, just remember it is a real dome. And it's the only one like it!

Howard Marx, M.D., Plastic Surgeon. Same dome as the comic "Over the hill and losing it." $12.00 – 15.00. A glass globe for Wall Drug, a drug store in South Dakota that is also something of a tourist attraction. $8.00 – 10.00.

KLOS 95.5 — Mark and Brian are DJs of this Los Angeles radio station. These domes were given out as prizes during the holidays. $18.00 – 22.00. Larchmont Engineering, manufacturers of artificial snow in the Boston area. $18.00 – 20.00.

Coca-Cola® — woman holding bottle of Coke. $12.00 – 15.00. Ace Architects — large dome with many buildings including Figaro, an Italian gelati restaurant, a San Francisco office building, the Snake building in Berkeley, the Flying Cow building on Pier 39, a condo on Telegraph Hill, and Leviathan, an early version of Ace's office. Ace Architects has its offices in Oakland, California. The dome was made in 1989 and designed by David Weingarten. $15.00 – 20.00.

Atlantic Scaffold and Ladder Co. This 1950s globe is filled with an oily liquid that doesn't freeze. The background has a wonderful deco look. Note the phone number with a letter exchange. $60.00 – 70.00.

Kan-Der Advertising Specialties — "Don't monkey around." Glass globe; oily liquid. $35.00 – 45.00. Gordon Hart Truck Line — moving truck on plastic base. $35.00 – 45.00.

BOTTOM LEFT: Globe for Western American Insurance Company. $35.00 – 45.00.

BOTTOM RIGHT: Greetings from Harry Stanley, a publishing company. $35.00 – 45.00. Skelly — "Your Surety of Service," tubeless tire company. $35.00 – 45.00.

LEFT: Texaco, with combination city and country background. The name of the dealer is advertised on the red base. $60.00 – 70.00.

RIGHT: White Star Trucking, Inc. The gold crown is less common than a truck. $65.00 – 75.00.

Newsweek. Large dome from 1990; red bars that say "Newsweek," as well as snow, swirl around when the dome is shaken. $60.00 – 70.00.

New York Times promotional dome from 1987. It has the logo of the Business Day section with a bear and a bull on a seesaw. The caption reads "One constant in an ever-changing market." Scarce. $100.00 up.

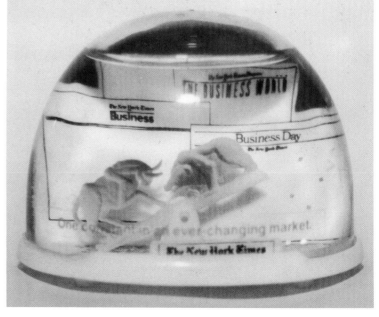

Nickelodeon (part of Universal network). Blimp shooting green slime on houses below. $12.00 – 15.00. Filmex, a now defunct movie agency; you can just make out the famous HOLLYWOOD sign in the background. There is a long pink Cadillac, beautiful people, and of course, a photographer! $25.00 – 28.00. Television's Greatest Hits produced a series of recordings of TV's most popular theme songs. $10.00 – 12.00.

Die Hard 2; part of a promotional gift at the preview. $22.00 – 26.00. Iran Air — prototype. $15.00 – 18.00.

Rollershop, a Vespa shop. $12.00 – 15.00. Air Canada. $14.00 – 16.00.

American Express Vacations — front and back view of same dome. $14.00 – 16.00.

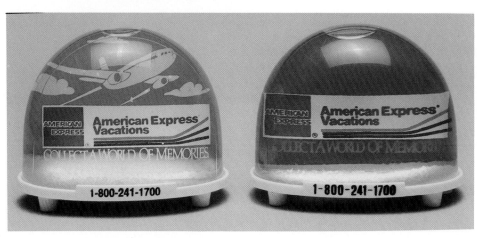

Abbeville Press — *Snowdomes* by Nancy McMichael; snow domes given to book dealers and at book fairs to publicize the book. Dome courtesy of Walton Rawls, editor. $12.00 – 16.00.

IBM computer, prototype. $22.00 – 25.00. Weitwelt, world-wide travel service. $10.00 – 12.00.

Urie's, Wildwood, New Jersey, a fish-fry restaurant. $8.00 – 10.00. Casa Bonita, a restaurant in Colorado. $8.00 – 10.00.

Reisebüro Rabenau — travel company. $10.00 – 12.00. Knorr, a Swiss soup mix company (double sided dome). $12.00 – 15.00.

Straßenwacht — street watch. $12.00 – 15.00.

Plahn. $10.00 – 12.00. Confetti, a boutique celebrating its fifth year in business. The saying means "Hello to friends" (thanks to Sherri Victor). $12.00 – 15.00.

Grone, Seit 1895. A private primary school. $12.00 – 15.00. Bronner's, year-round Christmas store in Frankenmuth, Michigan. $10.00 – 14.00.

Club Aldiana, Mulbach, Austria. A private resort. $12.00 – 15.00.

Wabco, hydraulic brake manufacturer. Slogan says, "Brake problems are like last night's snow to us." $12.00 – 14.00. Kleber — tire company. $10.00 – 14.00.

Swissôtel — lucite disc, made in Germany, hotel chain. $8.00 – 10.00. ZDF — newer dome with lucite disc. $8.00 – 10.00.

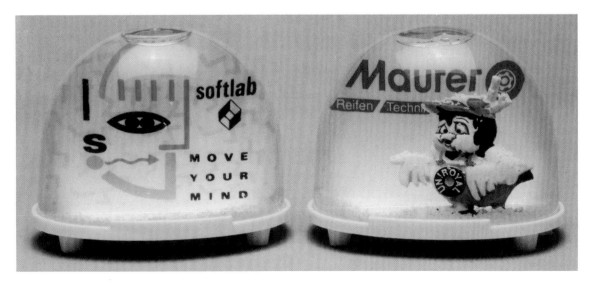

Softlab — software company. $8.00 – 10.00. Maurer — Reifen Technic Service, penguin with Uniroyal tire. $10.00 – 12.00.

Pritt Klebestift by Henkel — glue stick. $10.00 – 14.00. AGA Frigoscandia — two trucks, logo and building, trucking company. $12.00 – 15.00.

Radio FFH — Wir Kommen Rüber, Herzlichen Gluckwunsch (on reverse side in red "We are coming across with good wishes from the heart"). "Snow" is confetti. $12.00 – 15.00. Bonn ist 2000 — Ich bin dabei. "O" in Bonn is a lipstick print. Snow inside and three fat red stars. Celebration of Bonn's 2000th birthday. $12.00 – 15.00.

RIAS TV shows 3-D camera man behind TV camera, logo in back. A German TV station. $12.00 – 15.00. PPS — Photo Technik International; name on back. One taking picture and the other holding flash. Photo company. $12.00 – 15.00.

Grillo Spazzaneve, snow blowing service (Italian?). $12.00 – 15.00. Das Rosa Rote Jahr Der Bahn. Promotional fare of 99 Dm. offered on German railway (Die Bahn). $12.00 – 15.00.

Flamingo Productions film company. $14.00 – 16.00. Bavaria Filmstadt German film festival. $12.00 – 15.00.

Big Bang Schtroumpf — defunct amusement park, character was mascot. $15.00 – 18.00. DINGSDA — TV station. $12.00 – 15.00.

WDR-man in front of building, TV show personality. The building is Villa Hammerschmidt, the offficial residence of the German federal president. Perhaps the man is a reporter. $12.00 – 15.00. WDR Bei-Bio on seesaw, TV show. $12.00 – 15.00.

Franz Klammer. Background behind skiers says "schnee" (snow) printed over and over. Ski-wear company. $12.00 – 15.00. Cine Rent Köln — movie rental equipment company in Dusseldorf, Germany. $12.00 – 15.00.

CHARACTER DOMES

These charater domes are wonderful — and they appeal to two different collector groups: snow-dome and character collectibles.

Black and white Mickey and Minnie made by Bully in 1977, Walt Disney Company. $15.00 – 18.00 each.

Little Mermaid, Disney Collection. Bully, Germany. $15.00 – 18.00. Betty Boop by Bully, Germany. 1986, King Features Syndicate, Inc. Fleischer Studios, Inc. $15.00 – 18.00.

TOP AND CENTER: Ninja Turtles — Christmas, 1990. International Silver Co. Mirage Studios, USA. "Exclusively licensed by Surge Licensing Inc." Made in China. Leonardo, Donatello, Michaelangelo, and Raphael — all ready for Christmas! $12.00 – 15.00 each.

Mickey with Noel book — Kurt Adler. $12.00 – 15.00. Donald Duck as Santa — Walt Disney Company. $12.00 – 15.00.

Mickey on red heart — Koziol, West Germany. $15.00 – 18.00. Mickey on yellow base — Monogram Products, Largo, Florida. W.D. Productions. $20.00 – 22.00.

Mickey and Minnie, large oval dome. W.D. Productions. $22.00 – 25.00. The Wonderful World of Disney (Mickey and Minnie). Mickey and Donald (large oval dome). $22.00 – 25.00 each.

Felix the Cat — 1987. Licensor: Determined Productions; licensee: Standing Ovations. $12.00 – 15.00.

Smile — Bully, Germany. $12.00 – 15.00.

Snow White in glass globe atop house. W.D. Company. Music box plays "Some Day My Prince Will Come." $40.00 new.

The Flintstones — Hanna Barbera Productions, Inc. 1975. Fred, Pebbles, Bam Bam and Dino. Gateway says "Bedrock City." $22.00 – 25.00. Florida Orange Bird, older dome, three dimensional. $18.00 – 22.00.

Snoopy by Charles Schulz, three domes. Willits, 1966. $15.00 – 20.00 each.

Paul Bunyan and his blue ox Babe. $12.00 – 15.00. Babar the Elephant, storybook character by Jean de Brunhoff. $12.00 – 15.00.

Mickey Mouse, two different poses. $12.00 – 15.00 each.

Donald as Santa, $12.00 – 15.00. Pinocchio. $15.00 – 18.00.

Minnie and Mickey. $10.00 – 15.00 each.

Large dome — The Nutcracker. $10.00 – 15.00. The Wizard of Oz — all characters in one large dome. $12.00 – 15.00.

Disney characters in glass globes on wood base. 1988, Kurt Adler.

TOP: Pluto. $10.00 – 15.00. Clarabelle. $10.00 – 15.00.

BOTTOM: Goofy. $10.00 – 15.00. One of Snow White's dwarves. $10.00 – 15.00.

Jiminy Cricket. $10.00 – 15.00. Mickey as the Sorcerer's Apprentice. $12.00 – 15.00.

Mickey as Santa on chimney — music box plays "Santa Claus is Coming to Town." $18.00 – 22.00.

Oscar the Grouch (green) and Cookie Monster (blue) from the Sesame Street Muppets. Bottom says "Jim Henson Productions." $8.00 – 10.00.

Small Universal Studios dome — Chilly Willy and snowman on seesaw; Woody Woodpecker on back panel. $8.00 – 10.00. Universal Studios — skyline of New York, King Kong in background. $8.00 – 10.00. Universal Studios — divers on seesaw, Jaws in background. $8.00 – 10.00.

Marilyn Monroe — large glass dome. $35.00.

Charlie Chaplin. Enesco made this, the Marilyn Monroe dome, and Elvis with records floating around instead of snow. Chaplin was also represented in a musical jack-in-the-box, as a musical doll, and as an automated doll. The occasion, in 1989, was the hundredth anniversary of Chaplin's birth. The figure in the Chaplin dome is a better likeness than the one of Marilyn. $35.00.

Mickey in space suit. Globe contains both snow and stars. This dome would appeal to three different collectors: space, Mickey Mouse, and snow dome. Monogram Products; Largo, Florida, $40.00 – 45.00. Merry Kissmas. Ziggy, Universal Press Syndicate, 1980. $6.00 – 8.00.

Donald Duck. Schmid, 1989. The Walt Disney Co., made in China, printed in Hong Kong. $8.00 – 10.00.

Popeye — "You're one of a kind" 1989, made in China. This and the Teenage Mutant Ninja Turtle ink stamp dome are from the collection of my grandson, Jaime Guarnaccia, age 6. $8.00 – 10.00 each. The center dome in this photo is of Elmer Fudd, Warner Bros. He has a beehive in his hands and the "snow" is swarming bees. The caption says "oops!" $6.00 – 8.00.

CITIES AND STATES

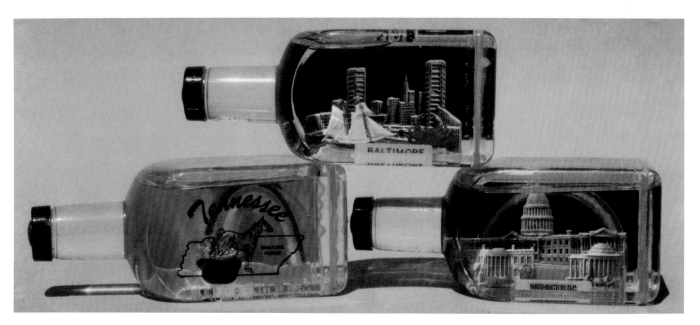

Many "domes" were and still are made in the shape of bottles. These cannot be refilled.

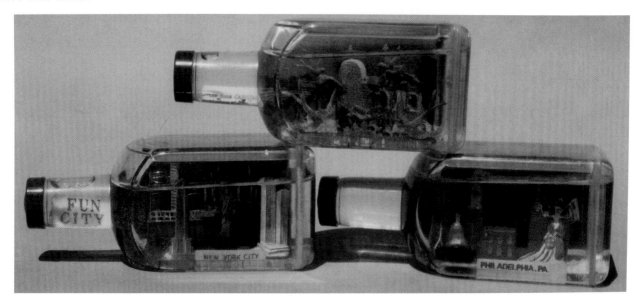

Fun City, New York City, San Juan Capistrano, and Philadelphia, Pennsylvania. $8.00 – 10.00 each.

Two domes from Washington, D.C. The most common domes are those from Washington, New York City, and San Francisco, probably because they attract more tourists than any other cities. $8.00 – 10.00 each.

Hollywood, Nashville, and Chicago. An unfortunate economy measure in making new domes is the use of a lucite disc with a decal for the background. Both the Hollywood bottle and the Nashville dome have this disc, although the Nashville dome does have some cut-out figures of country musicians forming a plaque in the foreground. $6.00 – 8.00 each.

TOP: Plymouth, Massachusetts. This dome has several individual figures: the Mayflower, Plymouth Rock (should be 1620), and an Indian. $8.00 – 10.00. Boston, Massachusetts, with the ubiquitous rainbow in the background. $8.00 – 10.00.

CENTER: A great dome from Nashville, showing a large hat and small cowboy. $10.00 – 12.00. Memphis. The black dome is a relative newcomer. Again, this dome has a decal on a lucite disc showing the Memphis skyline and has a plastic plaque of a Mississippi river boat in the foreground. $6.00 – 8.00.

BOTTOM: Salt Lake City. Good color and detail of mountains and skyline. $8.00 – 10.00.

Two domes from Chicago — in the dome on the right even the name of the city is a decal on a lucite plaque. $6.00 – 8.00 each.

Sacramento — a nice dome with steam train and capitol building. $8.00 – 10.00. Los Angeles — movie camera (what else?) on a seesaw. $20.00 – 22.00.

Philadelphia and New York City — the older New York domes, of course, would not show the World Trade Center, built 1974. $8.00 – 10.00 each.

San Francisco and Baltimore. Neither of these domes has the lucite disc. $8.00 – 10.00 each.

Atlanta with decal and St. Louis. $6.00 – 8.00 each.

This is a nice dome from Monterey showing the cypress tree and a lighthouse with a sea otter floating in a moving slot. $10.00 – 12.00. A good dome from Washington, D.C. with several separate plaques showing the major buildings. $10.00 – 12.00.

TOP: Two New York City domes featuring the Statue of Liberty. $10.00 – 12.00 each.

CENTER: There are many domes in this oval shape with a bright blue background. The one from Plymouth has the same interior as the oval dome; the dome on the right is from Fall River, Massachusetts and shows the USS Massachusetts. $10.00 – 12.00 each.

BOTTOM: Two treasure chests from Las Vegas — another popular variation of the dome shape. In some of these the dice move. $10.00 – 12.00.

Reno, Nevada with a cowboy at the gate to the city; Las Vegas featuring the Gold Nugget and the Mint. $10.00 – 12.00 each.

Two calendar domes. These look nice lined up as a separate or sub-collection. The one on the right, Las Vegas, has the months in twice instead of the days, and one side is upside down. $15.00 – 20.00. New Orleans. $15.00 – 20.00.

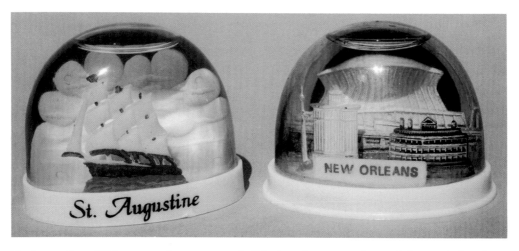

St. Augustine. This same three masted ship has been used to celebrate Columbus, for Martinique and Puerto Rico, and probably many others. When the name is painted on the outside of the dome, the same inside can and does serve many places. $6.00 – 8.00. New Orleans — this dome is so much nicer since the buildings in it and the paddle boat definitely belong to New Orleans. $8.00 – 10.00.

Here are some examples of generic domes; although the name of the city is on a plaque on the inside, the domes are otherwise identical.

Reno, Denver. $6.00 – 8.00 each.

Las Vegas, Cincinnati. $6.00 – 8.00 each.

Baltimore and Texas (sorry, not a city!). $6.00 – 8.00 each.

Seattle, USA — a topical collection, of ships, for instance, would be interesting to assemble. $6.00 – 8.00.

Collecting all 50 states is a challenge, and has been accomplished by some collectors. Unfortunately, I only have 42 states shown here, but the others exist.

Alabama: the State Capitol and Alaska with dog sled. $8.00 – 10.00.

These three domes from Alaska are newer but show, I think, how the increase in tourism there has led to an increase in production of domes. $8.00 – 10.00 each.

Arizona with cactus and a roadrunner. $6.00 – 8.00. Arkansas with a razorback and a man on seesaw. $8.00 – 10.00. Many states have a yellow outline map in the background, and show state animal, bird, and/or flower.

A new dome from California — black with a lucite disc, but I liked the design of the sun anyway. $6.00 – 8.00. Colorado with the pot of gold at the end of the rainbow, and outline of state map showing cities and rivers. $6.00 – 8.00.

Florida is a popular tourist place as are California and New York City. Each has many, many snow domes. This is a large dome with oranges, gulls and palm trees, and the only snow they'll ever see! $6.00 – 8.00. Georgia with the Confederate flag and peaches. $8.00 – 10.00.

Hawaii and Idaho. $8.00 – 10.00 each.

Iowa — small dome, state map in yellow and three Indians dancing in the front. This was a prototype made to see if there would be enough demand for them. There apparently was not, so they were never mass-produced. Scarce. $18.00 – 22.00. Indiana — famous for the Indy 500 race. $10.00 – 12.00.

Kansas — pine trees and buffalo. $8.00 – 10.00. Kentucky — seesaw with log cabin and horse, Capitol in background. $8.00 – 10.00.

Louisiana — state map in yellow with lobster, pelican and boat. $10.00 – 12.00. Oklahoma — black dome, lucite disc; Indians on horseback and mountains. $6.00 – 8.00.

LEFT: Maryland — rainbow, State house, crab and schooner. $10.00 – 12.00.

RIGHT: Massachusetts — the Mohawk Trail and Indian head on a lucite disc. $6.00 – 8.00.

Michigan — outline map, lighthouse and sailboat. $6.00 – 8.00. Maine — lighthouse with ring-toss game. $6.00 – 8.00. Montana — cowboys on horseback and mountains. $8.00 – 10.00.

Mississippi — state capitol. $8.00 – 10.00. Minnesota — large dome with rainbow and loon; plaque says "Common loon — state bird." $12.00 – 14.00.

New Mexico — lucite disc with Indians and adobe houses. $6.00 – 8.00. New Jersey — sailboat. $8.00 – 10.00.

Nebraska — barn and farm scene. $8.00 – 10.00. New Hampshire — lucite disc, covered bridge. $6.00 – 8.00.

North Carolina — yellow map, red bird. $6.00 – 8.00. Nevada — mountain background, miner pulling mule. $10.00 – 12.00.

Oregon — spotted fawn in front of lake (sticker says Made in China). $10.00 – 12.00. South Carolina — yellow map, red bird and state house. $10.00 – 12.00.

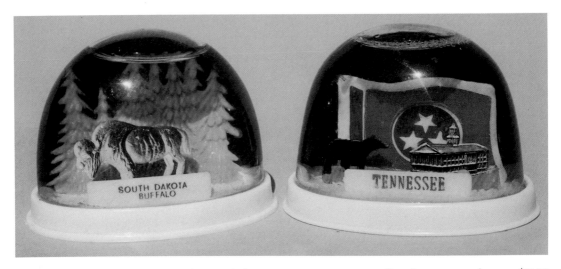

South Dakota — this is the identical dome to Kansas except for the name plaque. $8.00 – 10.00. Tennessee — state flag, Capitol building and black bear. $10.00 – 12.00.

Texas — yellow map; cowboy roping a jackalope. $10.00 – 12.00. Utah — this is a nice dome with the skier in front of Bryce Canyon and the Mormon Tabernacle. $10.00 – 12.00.

Virginia — yellow map, red bird, and flowers. $8.00 – 10.00. Vermont — deer in front of covered bridge. $6.00 – 8.00.

Washington — Elk with mountains and water. $8.00 – 10.00. West Virginia — black dome, lucite disc. Map is red with black bear in foreground. $6.00 – 8.00.

Ohio — same dome as Michigan except for map and name plaque. $6.00 – 8.00. Wisconsin. $8.00 – 10.00.

Wyoming — almost the same dome as Montana. $8.00 – 10.00.

DUAL-PURPOSE DOMES

Examples of combination snow dome and salt and pepper shakers. These appeal to two different categories of collectors.

Tall, "popsicle" shaped domes — Florida. The opaque chamber in the back holds the salt and pepper, the front is the snow dome. $15.00 – 20.00 pair.

Same shape — Washington, D.C. $15.00 – 20.00 pair.

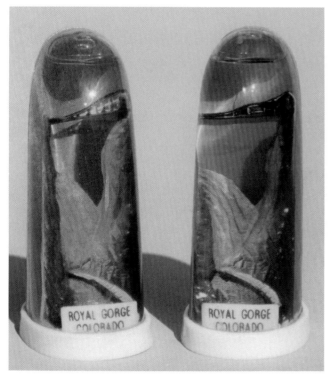

Royal Gorge, Colorado. This location is far less common than either Florida or Washington, D.C. $25.00 – 30.00 pair.

Another pair of Florida domes; these are both flamingos. $15.00 – 20.00 pair.

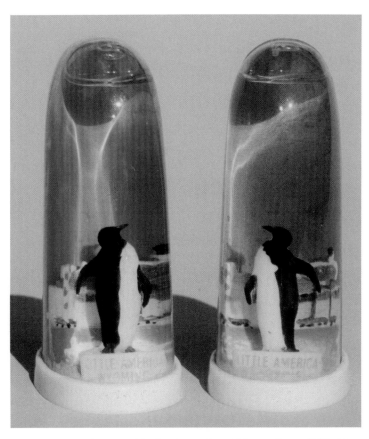

**Great Penguins — Little America, Wyoming. $25.00 –
30.00 pair.**

**The name on these shaker domes is printed on the
side: The Ozarks. $20.00 – 25.00 pair.**

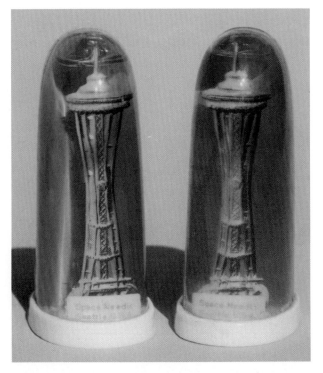

**Space Needle, Seattle, Washington. $15.00 –
20.00 pair.**

The following sets of salt and pepper domes are shaped like little TVs. There are two types: two separate pieces form the pair, with the snow at one end and the salt and pepper chamber at the other; or a one piece shaker with chambers for salt and pepper at either end and the snow in the middle.

Niagara Falls. $20.00 – 25.00 pair.

Florida. $15.00 – 20.00 pair.

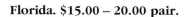

Florida. $15.00 – 20.00 pair.

Los Angeles Civic Center and Grauman's Chinese Theater, L.A. $25.00 – 30.00 pair.

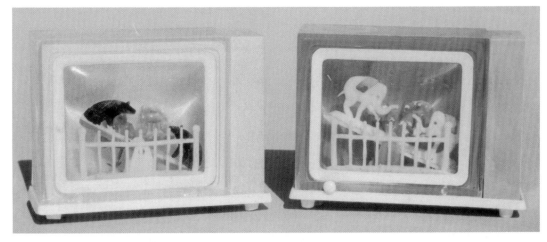

These have been used for many different zoos; this pair has no plaque, and may be a blank made to be labeled later. $20.00 – 30.00 pair.

Hawaii — girl in one; boy in the other. Knobs missing on one. $25.00 – 35.00 pair.

This is a one-piece shaker. The top slides to release the salt and pepper. This is an advertising shaker for Sears Kenmore Washer and Dryer. Of course, when you shake it, it looks like soap suds instead of snow. $40.00 – 50.00.

Canada. $20.00 – 25.00.

Great Smoky Mountains — two separate domes. $25.00 – 30.00 each.

A souvenir water globe in the original box, showing how to fill with salt and pepper. $30.00 – 35.00. Hearst Castle, San Simeon, California. $20.00 – 25.00.

Two Christmas salt and pepper/snow dome combinations. These are the most common, and so the easiest to find. $12.00 – 15.00 each.

Worlds of Fun and Sydney Harbor Bridge, Australia. $25.00 – 30.00 each.

This set is for salt, pepper, and sugar. $30.00 – 35.00 set.

Wonderful display of Teenage Mutant Ninja Turtles stamp domes. These have an ink stamp on the bottom. $6.00 – 8.00 each.

These are pencil toppers (shown in tooth-brush holder): Excalibur Hotel and Casino, Las Vegas. $6.00 – 8.00. Happy Holidays with Santa in the dome. $6.00 – 8.00.

ABOVE AND BELOW: More pencil twirlers — the Simpsons. $6.00 – 8.00 each.

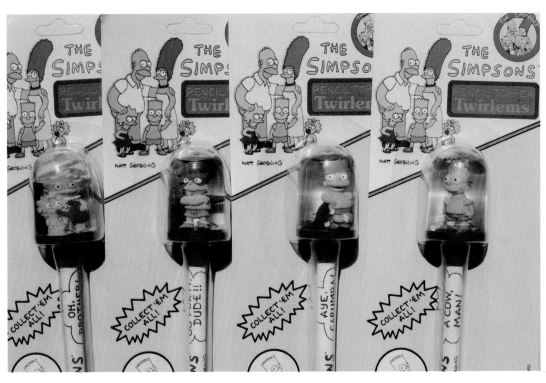

Calendar based domes, another category of domes with a dual purpose. Washington, D.C. and Hearst Castle. $20.00 – 22.00 each.

The Night Before Christmas — Santa's World. $15.00 – 20.00. Dutch Wonderland, Lancaster, Pennsylvania. $10.00 – 15.00.

TOP: DeHart pen holder. A glass advertising globe. $35.00 – 45.00.

CENTER LEFT: Glass and Bakelite ashtray dome from Yellowstone Park. $45.00 – 55.00.

CENTER RIGHT: Another glass and Bakelite ashtray dome from Yellowstone, this time with a bear. $45.00 – 55.00.

BOTTOM LEFT: A Snow Baby in a glass dome on a Bakelite ashtray. $65.00 – 75.00.

BOTTOM RIGHT: A pink Florida ashtray, glass and plastic. $35.00 – 45.00.

There are combination snow domes and toys. Here a working kaleidoscope has a snow dome in the base and a music box in the bottom. Really multi-purpose! Made by Silvestri, the music box plays "Santa Claus is Coming to Town." $25.00 – 35.00.

These three domes have animals that open their mouths when the dome is inverted. The object of the game is to catch the "snow" in the animal's mouth. $6.00 – 8.00 each.

There are loads of snow domes with ring toss games: I guess it's not enough just to sit and watch the snow fall! Bottles with vertical figures to catch the rings. $6.00 – 9.00 each.

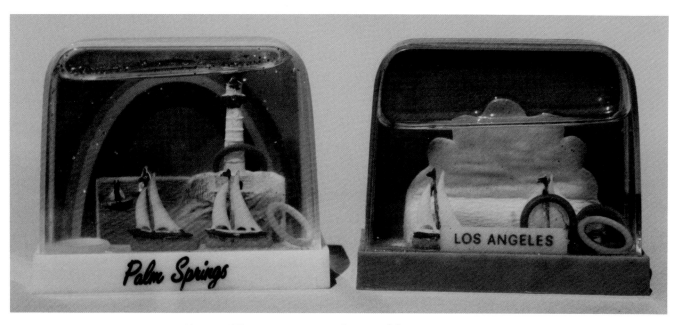

Two California ring toss domes. $6.00 – 8.00 each.

Cape Hatteras, Florida and Gulf Shores — all with rings. $6.00 – 8.00 each.

San Francisco, a dinosaur, and Sea World — more ring toss. $6.00 – 8.00 each.

Florida and San Francisco are very common. $6.00 – 8.00 each. Panama City Beach is more unusual than the other two. $8.00 – 10.00.

Ring toss bottles — Key West, and more from Florida. $6.00 – 7.00 each.

A snow dome with a pencil sharpener in the bottom — Niagara Falls, Canada. $10.00 – 12.00.

Water ball pin-on card; this dome is not only jewelry, but it spins as well. Made in China. $8.00 – 10.00.

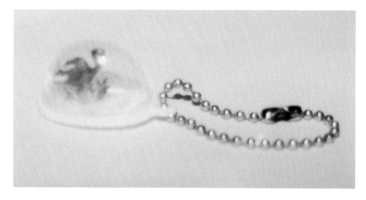

Key chain with a snow dome a mere ¾" containing a flamingo. $8.00 – 10.00.

FIGURAL DOMES

These Santas may all look alike, but there are variations.

These two Santas are very similar except for the green bag, but the images inside are completely different. $15.00 – 18.00 each.

Each of these Santas has a deer over his shoulders. $15.00 – 18.00 each.

Very scarce clown. $75.00 – 100.00. Elf. Looks like one of Santa's helpers. Why aren't there more of them than of Santas? $75.00 – 100.00.

The figural Santa on the left is unusual because it is on a square base. The one on the right is by Brite Star Mfg. $15.00 – 18.00 each.

A church, a tree and a mountain, all containing water balls within them. $22.00 – 25.00 each.

These Santas have very wrinkled brows. $15.00 – 20.00 each.

A sitting Santa. $18.00 – 20.00. A standing Santa. $15.00 – 18.00.

The previous figural Santas were all plastic; this one is ceramic, and the ball is glass. Midwest Imports. $28.50 new.

These two Santas are quite elaborate; the textured porcelain is fashioned to make them look old, but they are not. $20.00 – 25.00 each.

Back to plastic: Santa on a chimney, and holding a lantern. $18.00 – 20.00 each.

Mr. and Mrs. Santa atop chimneys, different scenes inside. $18.00 – 20.00 each.

Two more ceramic snowmen — the one on the left is part of a very elaborate group, with a nice clear image inside the globe. $20.00 – 25.00 each.

This tall snowman is nicely crafted of ceramic. Applause, 1988. $15.00 – 18.00.

Two boxes tied with bows, plastic. $12.00 – 15.00 each.

Three "lanterns." I find figural shapes more interesting than the oval domes. $15.00 – 18.00 each.

A plastic boot, a child atop a dome, and a coffeepot. $12.00 – 15.00 each.

These plastic figurals are quite detailed for the relatively low price. $18.00 – 20.00 each.

These two snowmen have marshmallow looking faces. Lots going on inside the water balls. $15.00 – 20.00 each.

70

Two very jolly snowmen. $15.00 – 18.00 each.

The clown-like snowman on the left has no arms. The inside shows two children running around Christmas trees. $15.00 – 18.00. The snowman on the right is a rocker, with a child on each side for balance. $18.00 – 20.00.

These three snowmen are all alike, but their insides are different. $15.00 – 20.00 each.

The Halloween domes have bats flying around inside (in the belfry?). The figural witch is a lovely shade of green. Inside the globe an owl, a ghost and a pumpkin are offering "best witches." $15.00 – 18.00 each.

The generic alligator with seesaw inside. I have seen these from many different locations. $10.00 – 12.00 each.

Three great frogs: plastic, and all from different places. $12.00 – 15.00 each.

TOP AND CENTER: There are many animals atop domes. The same dome was used to depict many places. The seesaw inside is very common. Monkey, bear and lion. $15.00 – 18.00 each.

The dolphin atop dome is also ubiquitous. The first one of these that I saw was at Cedar Point, Ohio, an amusement park where they certainly do not have dolphins! $12.00 – 15.00 each.

Black bear, 1972 Smoky Mountains. UVC Inc. $20.00 – 25.00. The panda from Canada presides over a globe with two small pandas playing in the grass. Note position of feet on bear and panda — the same except for coloring. $20.00 – 25.00.

Tiger and elephant. This elephant has nice detail and realistic looking wrinkled skin — there is a newer one out that is smooth and less detailed. $15.00 – 18.00 each.

An orange from Florida, $15.00 – 18.00. An orange fish, $25.00 – 30.00.

Weeki Wachee is a water sport resort in Florida. Mermaid. $15.00 – 18.00. Parrots inside globe are being watched by a bright yellow parrot on the outside. This globe was made in China. $18.00 – 20.00.

The red hearts stand for "I love New York" and Toronto. $12.00 – 14.00 each.

This girl with the snowman is very strange — there's absolutely nothing in the globe but water and a tiny bit of glitter. $14.00 – 16.00.

An apple for the teacher. $8.00 – 10.00.

These two seamen are wonderful. The one on the left is from the Queen Mary, Long Beach, California. The other says Carowinds. $35.00 – 40.00 each.

Bugs Bunny. $85.00 – 95.00.

Mickey Mouse. $75.00 – 85.00. Pinocchio. $85.00 – 95.00. These are fabulous and relatively scarce. Mickey is a little easier to find than the others.

Bottom of Pinocchio showing the Disney mark.

Blarney Beer. $8.00 – 10.00. Seated Irishman with pot o' gold. $15.00 – 18.00.

This great dome has two seamen with one globe. It is from Germany. $35.00 – 45.00.

FOREIGN DOMES

Poster from Grimentz, Switzerland. Carol Hofflich, a collector from Fairfield, Connecticut, found this poster in this charming Swiss village in the Office of Tourism. They had a dome made up very similar to the dome in the poster, and it looks just like the village, where the houses all have window boxes full of red geraniums. This is a skiing and hiking resort.

Grimentz and Schilthorn — the latter a 2970 meter mountain in Switzerland. $14.00 – 18.00 each.

I love Gstaad — Switzerland. $14.00 – 16.00. A herder and his cow; Switzerland is printed both inside and outside the dome and the Swiss flag is right in the middle. $12.00 – 15.00.

Lucerne — this is the famous covered bridge across the lake. $15.00 – 18.00. Mauritius is an island in the South Pacific near Indonesia. The dome was purchased in Florida. $30.00 – 40.00.

TOP LEFT AND RIGHT, AND CENTER: Lausanne — this is an unusual two-sided dome. One side shows "Ouchy" the waterfront; the other shows the old city. $15.00 – 18.00.

This dome that says Europe contains the 12 flags of the Common Market countries. $12.00 – 14.00.

Versailles — the dome shows the palace and the gardens. $15.00 – 18.00. Côte D'Azur, $10.00 – 12.00.

Carcassonne — walled city in France on the Canal du Midi. $12.00 – 15.00. Chamonix — Mt. Blanc is the tallest mountain in Europe; this is a generic dome — they write the name in front. $8.00 – 10.00.

Another dome from Chamonix. $8.00 – 10.00. Annecy — another town in France. These domes have plugs on the top. $10.00 – 12.00.

Moulin de Daudet, town in Provence. $12.00 – 15.00. Mont St. Michel claims to be the home of the omelet. The land is flat and the church is built up high. $10.00 – 12.00.

La Rochelle calendar base — in French, of course! $15.00 – 18.00. Paris, the Eiffel Tower. $18.00 – 22.00.

Pont d'Avignon, the town in Provence, southern France, immortalized in song. $15.00 – 18.00. Les Baux de Provence, a beautiful walled town, $15.00 – 18.00.

Lyon, a city in France. $12.00 – 15.00. Another dome from Mt. St. Michel. $15.00 – 18.00.

Two calendar domes from Paris featuring the Eiffel Tower. $15.00 – 18.00 each.

Liechtenstein. $10.00 – 12.00. Holland — two children on see-saw. $10.00 – 12.00.

Souvenir of Luxembourg. $12.00 – 15.00. St. Peter's Cathedral in Rome. $12.00 – 15.00.

Geneva and Bern, both cities in Switzerland. These are new domes, made in Germany. $10.00 – 12.00 each.

Eilat, Israel. $18.00 – 20.00. Jerusalem. $15.00 – 18.00.

Denmark with a Viking ship. $10.00 – 12.00. Copenhagen with the little mermaid that sits in the harbor. $12.00 – 15.00.

Two domes from Australia. The opera house in Sydney. $15.00 – 18.00. A kangaroo and a koala. $15.00 – 18.00.

Berlin Tut Gut. The three dimensional bear in front is the symbol of Berlin. $20.00 – 25.00. Neuschwanstein. Ludwig's castle in Bavaria was the model for Disneyland's castle. $10.00 – 12.00.

Ulm — city along the Danube (Donau) where Einstein was born. $15.00 – 20.00. Heidelberg, city on the Neckar river; oldest German university city. $12.00 – 15.00.

I Love Germany. Small German made dome. $10.00 – 12.00. Salzburg, Austria; inside plaque. $15.00 – 18.00. München (Munich) — child sitting on a beer keg. $15.00 – 18.00.

Steinerne Brücke, 1135 – 1985. $15.00 – 18.00. Kölner Dom — Cathedral of Cologne, Germany. $12.00 – 15.00. Stuttgart, an industrial town, home of Porsche and Mercedes. $12.00 – 15.00.

Sevilla, children as Flamenco dancers with La Giralda, the tower built by the Moors and still standing today. $12.00 – 15.00. Mijas, a town in southern Spain. $15.00 – 18.00.

The dome on the left is quintessential tacky — it's all plastic and has delusions of grandeur with its rose draperies and gold base. $20.00 – 25.00. A small common dome, souvenir of Pisa. $10.00 – 12.00.

Pisa — the famous tower and church. Many of the Italian domes have shells and stones encrusted on the base. $35.00 – 45.00.

Capri, famous blue grotto. $12.00 – 15.00. S. Gimignano, near Siena in Italy. The tall chimneys are a sign of affluence. $15.00 – 18.00.

Zoo Safari del Garda. This dome from Garda in Italy was bought in Brighton, England. $20.00 – 22.00. Lago di Garda is a beautiful resort area in Italy. $12.00 – 15.00.

Monteriggioni. $12.00 – 15.00. Venezia. The famous Bridge of Sighs in Venice; gondola in foreground. $10.00 – 12.00.

These domes from England are the bullet shape. From left to right: London Bobby (2), The Beefeater, and the Palace Guard (2). $8.00 – 10.00 each.

London Bridge and Parliament Buildings. $8.00 – 10.00. Trafalgar Square, London. Double decker red bus on left. $8.00 – 10.00.

Windsor Castle — the scene of a fire in 1992. $8.00 – 10.00. Tower Bridge, London. $8.00 – 10.00.

Windsor Castle palace guard. Queen Elizabeth's weekend home. $8.00 – 10.00. Isle of Wight car ferry. $12.00 – 15.00. A present from Brighton. Brighton is a beach resort south of London and does not have a zoo! $10.00 – 12.00.

Buckingham Palace, the royal residence in London. $8.00 – 10.00. London Zoo. $10.00 – 12.00.

Canada — The Royal Canadian Mounted Police. $12.00 – 14.00. Canadian flag, mountains, and RCMP. $10.00 – 12.00.

Victoria, British Columbia, Canada. Parliament buildings in background; moving boat in front. $10.00 – 12.00. Vancouver, Canada — moose in front of Canadian flag. $10.00 – 12.00.

Montreal-St. Joseph. $10.00 – 12.00. Large dome of Montreal stadium and skyline. $10.00 – 12.00.

Toronto-CN Tower. $10.00 – 12.00. Quebec — Le Chateau Frontenac, a beautiful, old world hotel. $10.00 – 12.00.

Toronto — new city hall. $8.00 – 10.00. Toronto — black dome with skyline and ferry. $10.00 – 12.00.

Ste. Anne de Beaupré, famous church in Montreal. $8.00 – 10.00. Niagara Falls, Canada, with boat "The Maid of the Mist." $10.00 – 12.00.

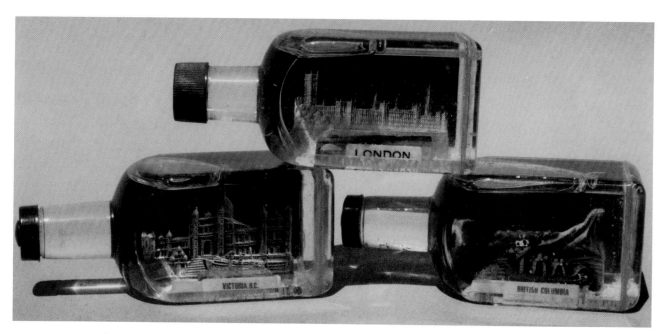

Bottles: London, England, Victoria, B.C. and British Columbia. $12.00 – 15.00 each.

GERMAN MADE DOMES

Many domes such as these were sold in gift shops in 1990. They are used for advertising and/or as souvenirs. The ones pictured here have no captions, but some of them appear, with captions, elsewhere in this book — such as the Vespa and the Knorr soup ad.

These are part of a series of nursery rhymes. A goat (Red Riding Hood?) and wolf. $10.00 – 12.00.
Puss in Boots. $10.00 – 12.00.

The Frog and the Princess. $10.00 – 12.00. Hansel and Gretel. $10.00 – 12.00.

Snow White and the Seven Dwarfs. $10.00 – 12.00. Red Riding Hood and the Wolf. $10.00 – 12.00.

Cinderella (Aschenputtel). $10.00 – 12.00. Das tapfere Schneiderlein (The Brave Little Tailor). $6.00 – 8.00.

Native American totem and tepees. $8.00 – 10.00. Cowboys and mountains. $8.00 – 10.00.

Drama masks and wine. $6.00 – 8.00. Photographers. $6.00 – 8.00.

Space man. $10.00 – 12.00. Santa on rocket. $10.00 – 15.00.

Deep sea diver on sea horse. $6.00 – 8.00. Blue fish, $6.00 – 8.00.

Girl walking on beach. $6.00 – 8.00. Girl on beach ball with sailboat. $6.00 – 8.00.

Man with pickaxe in cave. $6.00 – 8.00. Couple in cable car. $6.00 – 8.00.

Man on horse. This looks like a Lippizaner stallion and rider, of the Spanish Riding School in Vienna, Austria. $8.00 – 10.00. Bull and bull fighter. $8.00 – 10.00.

A different version of Hansel and Gretel. $8.00 – 10.00. Cinderella. $10.00 – 12.00.

Ice cream cone — this dome was used to advertise Waikiki Coolers. $8.00 – 10.00. Bacchus with grapes on keg of wine. $6.00 – 8.00.

Two ballerinas. $6.00 – 8.00 each.

Fish and porpoises. $6.00 – 8.00.

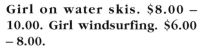

Steamship. $6.00 – 8.00. Sailboats. $8.00 – 10.00.

Girl on water skis. $8.00 – 10.00. Girl windsurfing. $6.00 – 8.00.

Camel. $6.00 – 8.00. Moose or elk — this or one very similar was used in Knorr soup ad. $10.00 – 12.00.

Ski-jumper. $10.00 – 12.00. Angel on skis. $8.00 – 10.00.

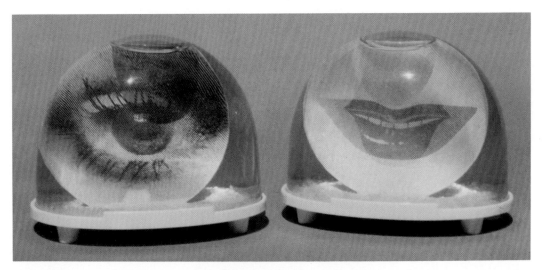

Eye and lips — winkies, or moving images similar to holograms. $10.00 – 12.00 each.

Goldfish. $6.00 – 8.00. Parrot. $6.00 – 8.00.

Motorcycle. $8.00 – 10.00. This dome was used for a Vespa ad. $6.00 – 8.00.

Girl on plastic float. $6.00 – 8.00. Convertible. $8.00 – 10.00.

Train. $6.00 – 8.00. Truck. $6.00 – 8.00.

GLASS DOMES

Glass domes, of course, came before plastic. The earliest known domes were made in the late nineteenth century, and the first ones made were used as paperweights. The snow globe was immortalized in the movie classic *Citizen Kane,* the great work of Orson Welles released in 1941.

In the opening of the film, Kane is lying in bed gazing at the snow falling on a house and snowman — all contained in a glass snow globe. He utters a single word, "Rosebud" and dies, dropping the glass globe which rolls down the steps and shatters. Rosebud refers to the sled of his childhood, which he remembers as he looks into the globe filled with snow.

Two snowmen in glass globes — the one on the left has a ceramic base, and the one on the right has a Bakelite base.

Two glass globes with a religious theme: St. Anthony on a Bakelite base and the Crucifix, with ceramic base made by Atlas Crystal Works, Trenton, New Jersey. $35.00 – 45.00 each.

Two figures — with skis (?). $20.00 – 25.00 each.

The Capitol Building, ceramic base, 1940s. $35.00 – 45.00. Black cat on Bakelite base. Cat has red bird on head. $35.00 – 40.00.

Rudolph the Red Nosed Reindeer, by the Driss Company, Chicago, Illinois. This has an almost perfect label — a consideration since the labels in this series are of paper and are on the outside. $35.00 – 45.00. Frosty the Snowman — good condition inside, but no label. $25.00 – 30.00.

The Lone Ranger — with both red and green plastic base — these are both in excellent condition and the water level is good; this is a factor, as these are very difficult to fill. They do not have a plug as do the plastic domes, and must be taken apart, always with the risk of breakage. $65.00 – 75.00 each.

Niagara Falls, glass on Bakelite base. The first time I saw this I thought that someone had inserted a cardboard picture of the falls in an empty globe. Then I saw others just like this. $30.00 – 35.00. Washington Monument, 1939. $35.00 – 45.00.

The Little Flower, St. Theresa, the Carmelite Nun, with flowers and a cross. $40.00 – 45.00. St. Francis Monastery — Portiuncula, Burlington, Wisconsin. $40.00 – 45.00.

CENTER: World War II Soldier — water level cut off head in photograph. 1940s. 40.00 – 45.00. General Douglas MacArthur — America's Hero. Atlas Crystal Works. Porcelain base, 1940s. $45.00 – 55.00.

BOTTOM LEFT: The George Washington Masonic National Memorial oil filled globe. 1950s. Plastic base. $30.00 – 40.00.

BOTTOM RIGHT: Washington's Home, Mount Vernon. $35.00 – 45.00. House with pine trees — Yosemite National Park. $35.00 – 45.00.

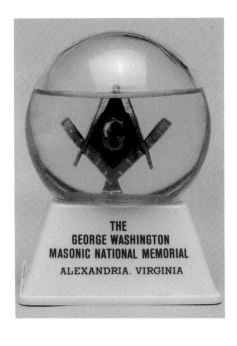

Black Bear — Sequoia National Park.
$40.00 – 45.00.

A snow baby type figure in a modern glass globe with wood base. $20.00 – 22.00.

A new glass dome from Willits — a beautiful globe of the U.S.S. Enterprise from *Star Trek*. This is the first in a series of three globes to be produced by Willits. *Star Trek* is a registered trademark of Paramount Pictures. $50.00.

North Pole, New York, home of Santa's Workshop. Oil filled, 1950s. $45.00 – 55.00.

This is a magnificent globe that belongs to Chloe Ross. It is of the Eiffel Tower. It has a small gold sticker that says "The Man in the Eiffel Tower," RKO Pictures Release. That movie came out in January 1950. $125.00 – 150.00.

Golfer who shakes up sand instead of snow — wood base. House and trees on painted wood base — music box plays Christmas carols. $20.00 – 25.00 each.

HOLIDAYS AND CELEBRATIONS

Valentine with slot for photo. $12.00 – 14.00.

Ceramic hand base with wonderful black nails. $30.00 – 35.00. Four small domes. $2.00 – 4.00 each.

Trick or treat globe with haunted house and witch. $8.00 – 10.00 each.

Large glass globe on painted wood base. Battery operated skull lights up and blinks. Base has "BOO" painted all around in orange. By Silvestri. $20.00 – 22.00. Large glass globe; wood base. Witch moon and witch cat. Enesco 1991. $20.00 – 22.00. Large glass globe; hand holding skull; Applause. $22.00 – 25.00.

Pumpkin shaped glass globe. Celebrations, Chicago, Illinois. $20.00 – 25.00. Skeleton with pumpkin. Midwest Imports of Canon Falls, Inc. $18.00 – 22.00.

Smaller domes — Boo ghost on spring atop pumpkin. $6.00 – 8.00. Cat on pumpkin — bats fly around instead of snow. Pacific Rim. $6.00 – 8.00. Tiny and not very frightening devil. $4.00 – 6.00.

Three more globes for Halloween; these change each year. Witch with green hands and face. $8.00 – 10.00. Skeleton seated on coffin with head in hand. $8.00 – 10.00. Vampire with orange cape. $8.00 – 10.00.

Dome with hat on the outside, owl and pumpkin inside — says "best witches." Enesco 1989, designed by Mark Cook. $10.00 – 12.00. Globe with haunted house and bats by Marcel Schurman Co., Inc., San Francisco. $6.00 – 8.00. Globe with three ghosts atop cut out pumpkin — Midwest Imports. $6.00 – 8.00.

There are several globes with rabbits and chicks. Many of these are by Enesco, and some by Dakin. Midwest Imports, 1988. $6.00 – 8.00.

Christmas domes are, of course, the most common of all the holiday domes.

Santa Claus in a flying saucer — this would appeal to space as well as to snow dome collectors. This dome lights up. Enesco 1990. $35.00 – 45.00.

Very large glass globe on ornate metal base. Santa with gnomes on sled. Music box plays "Santa Claus is Coming to Town"; Mercuries, USA. $25.00 – 30.00.

Two fairly ordinary Christmas domes with Santa, children, and snowmen. $6.00 – 8.00 each.

Donald going skiing. Glass globe, wood base. $8.00 – 10.00. Goofy, Mickey, Donald, and Minnie around the Christmas tree. Paper label says "Merry Christmas!" This dome must be re-issued every year, as I have seen it new in retail stores many times. Licensee is Kurt S. Adler Inc., New York, New York. From the Disney Character Collection, the Walt Disney Company. $8.00 – 10.00.

This Christmas dome has a string to pull that activates the snow. $8.00 – 10.00.

Bell-shaped domes. These could be hung from the tree. $8.00 – 10.00 each.

Pointed domes. 1980 Unieboek, B.V., a Dutch Company. $10.00 – 12.00 each.

These three domes say "fabrique en Chine" and so were probably made for France. They show Santa, a snowman, and an angel, sitting on the Concorde. Rare. $15.00 – 25.00 each.

Another figural Santa; this one is unusual as Santa is sitting in a rocket inside the globe. $30.00 – 35.00. Santa coming in over the rooftops in a rocket. $25.00 – 30.00.

Wedding domes — Good Luck and Weddingland. $8.00 – 10.00 each.

Happy Birthday. These could be given instead of greeting cards! $6.00 – 8.00 each.

Baby announcement — pink or blue? $6.00 – 8.00.

It's a boy, graduation, and a gift for a golf champ. $6.00 – 8.00 each.

New Arrival and Happy Birthday. $6.00 – 8.00 each.

This white rose was a favor given to all of the women at a wedding; the dome was given to me to photograph by Maria Santos. $6.00 – 8.00.

Greeting card domes. $6.00 – 8.00 each.

Have an ICE day! Let's Celebrate. $6.00 – 8.00 each.

HUMOROUS DOMES AND MISTAKES

A grouping of melted snowmen — all that's left is the top hat, carrot, and coal!

TOP: Older melted snowman dome — Florida. Top hat and cane are all that's left. $10.00 – 15.00 each.

CENTER: Contemporary melted snowman — these should be of warm climates where a snowman wouldn't last. I don't think the people in Boston or Cape Cod got the joke! $6.00 – 8.00 each.

BOTTOM: California Real Estate. $10.00 – 15.00. Los Angeles bottled smog (the "snow" is black). $10.00 – 15.00.

A series of six domes — a man (drunk?) trying to get up. He's wearing a black suit and hat and a bright red tie — in the first dome he's leaning against a red fire hydrant; he gets up, lands in a garbage can, gets up again, falls down, and finally, ends up on his back with his feet in the air. $25.00 – 30.00 for series.

Housework Sucks (so does the vacuum). Enesco 1989, Mark Cook, designer. $6.00 – 8.00. I took the plunge. Enesco 1989, Mark Cook, designer, made in China. $6.00 – 8.00.

Over the hill and losing 'em. Enesco 1990. $8.00 – 10.00. Over the hill and losing it, (this one was used by a plastic surgeon as an ad for hair implants). Enesco 1987. $8.00 – 10.00.

No loitering at cooler. $6.00 – 8.00.

As with coins or postage stamps, errors in printing do happen. Will these mistakes make the domes as valuable as a misprinted stamp? Only time will tell!

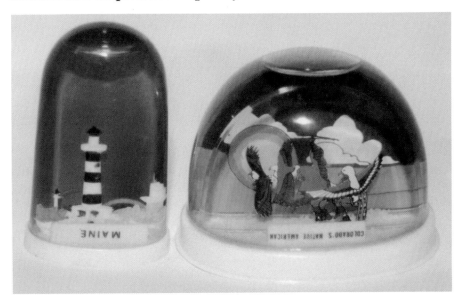

Maine — the plaque printed upside down. $20.00 – 25.00. Colorado's Native American — inverted plaque. $20.00 – 25.00.

These two domes have their name plaques switched: Franklin Institute, Philadelphia, Pennsylvania. $20.00 – 25.00. Pioneer Tunnel Coal Mine, Ashland, Pennsylvania. $20.00 – 25.00.

Colorado, Hollywood, and Natural Bridge, Virginia, all have inverted plaques. $20.00 – 25.00 each.

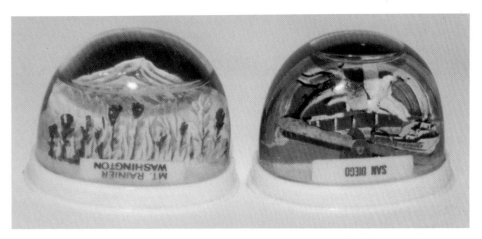

Mt. Rainier, Washington, and San Diego — inverted plaques. $20.00 – 25.00 each.

Florida — inverted name plaque. $15.00 – 20.00.

Gondola in Venezia and horse in Santa Cruz beach are both mounted with their painted side inward. $15.00 – 20.00 each.

Lancaster is misspelled; Michigan is in front of a map of Wisconsin. $12.00 – 15.00 each.

RELIGIOUS DOMES

These are pretty domes, with three dimensional figures, but somehow a plastic snowdome seems more kitsch than religious.

These tall narrow domes are made in Germany. Souvenir de Laghet. $12.00 – 14.00. Altotting — Black Madonna and Child seem to float above church. $8.00 – 10.00.

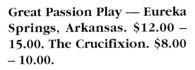

Un-named Saints. $8.00 – 10.00 each.

Great Passion Play — Eureka Springs, Arkansas. $12.00 – 15.00. The Crucifixion. $8.00 – 10.00.

Lourdes. $12.00 – 15.00. HL Dreifaltigkeit (Holy Trinity). Also German made. $8.00 – 10.00.

Fatima. $12.00 – 15.00. The Resurrection. $8.00 – 10.00.

The Christ of the Ozarks. $12.00 – 15.00. Israel. $15.00 – 18.00.

Two small domes of angels — (generic angels?). $8.00 – 10.00 each.

More religious domes depicting the birth and the Adoration. $8.00 – 10.00 each.

Two domes with children and priests; the center dome is of the Christ child with Mary and Joseph. $8.00 – 10.00 each.

Dickeyville Grotto, Dickeyville, Wisconsin. $8.00 – 10.00. Holy Hill, Hubertus, Wisconsin. $10.00 – 12.00.

Glorieta — the chapel at a very large and beautiful Baptist retreat outside of Santa Fe, New Mexico. $8.00 – 10.00. St. Mary's in the Mountains, Virginia City. $12.00 – 15.00.

Nuestra Señora de Coromoto — Patrona de Venezuela. $20.00 – 22.00. A Nativity with batteries, tiny light bulb inside. Some even pulsate! $18.00 – 22.00.

Montesenario — a shrine in Italy; the dome is encrusted with shells and stones. Very elaborate — on a mirror base. $35.00 – 40.00.

SPORTS DOMES

This is a sample of FanDomes made by the Kintra Group in Los Angeles, California. They are large domes, made for each team. These were prevalent in Cooperstown, New York, where the Baseball Hall of Fame is located.

COLLEGE FOOTBALL — SERIES #1, EDITION #1
University of Alabama, Crimson Tide — We're #1, University of Arizona, Wildcats — We're #1.
$6.00 – 8.00 each.

MAJOR LEAGUE BASEBALL — OFFICIAL LICENSE; SERIES #1, EDITION #2
St. Louis Cardinals, New York Yankees. $6.00 – 8.00 each.

Cincinnati Reds, Houston Astros. $6.00 – 8.00 each.

Pittsburgh Pirates, California Angels. $6.00 – 8.00 each.

NATIONAL FOOTBALL LEAGUE — SERIES #1, EDITION #1

Denver Broncos, Fightin' Irish — Notre Dame, Los Angeles Rams. $6.00 – 8.00 each.

Cincinnati Bengals, Chicago Bears. $6.00 – 8.00 each.

Los Angeles Raiders, Atlanta Falcons. $6.00 – 8.00 each.

Pittsburgh Steelers, San Francisco 49ers. $6.00 – 8.00 each.

Indianapolis Colts, Washington Redskins. $6.00 – 8.00 each.

NATIONAL HOCKEY LEAGUE — SERIES #1, EDITION #2

Los Angeles Kings, San José Sharks. $6.00 – 8.00 each.

BASKETBALL

Los Angeles Lakers, Chicago Bulls. $6.00 – 8.00 each.

TOURIST ATTRACTIONS

Tourist Attractions: amusement parks, beach resorts, historic buildings, military sites, national and state parks, caves, and natural wonders.

The Redwoods are a popular tourist attraction and the highway is the means to an end — the constant movement of people from one place to another — to explore, to learn, and to hunt — for snowdomes!

Olvera Street, Los Angeles. $8.00 – 10.00. Prehistoric Forest, Irish Hills. $10.00 – 15.00.

Both of these domes have a moving seesaw. Tombstone, Arizona. $8.00 – 10.00. Old Abilene Town, Abilene, Kansas. $12.00 – 15.00.

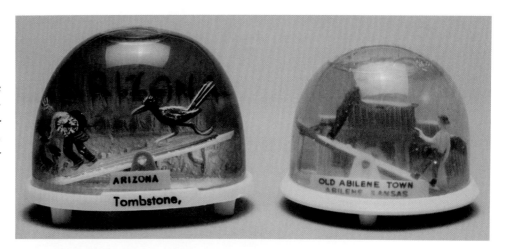

Ponderosa Ranch, Nevada. $12.00 – 15.00. Death Valley. $8.00 – 10.00. Hoover Dam. $8.00 – 10.00.

Space Farm. $8.00 – 10.00. Blue Ridge Parkway. $8.00 – 10.00.

Enchanted Forest, Maryland. $8.00 –
10.00. Another example from the
Enchanted Forest. $8.00 – 10.00.

Dutch Wonderland, Lancaster,
Pennsylvania. $8.00 – 10.00. San
Miguel Mission — Oldest Church
in USA. $12.00 – 15.00.

Santa Cruz. $8.00 – 10.00. South of the Border, South Carolina. $12.00 – 15.00.

Oroville Dam, California.
$12.00 – 15.00. Game
Haven, Wolverine, Michi-
gan. $12.00 – 15.00.

Six Flags over Texas. $12.00 – 15.00.
Six Flags — Magic Mountain. $12.00 –
15.00.

Two calendar domes with see-
saws: Six Flags over Georgia, and
Magic Mountain. $15.00 – 20.00
each.

Gingerbread Castle, Hamburg,
New Jersey. $8.00 – 10.00. Sto-
rybook Land, Cardiff, New Jersey. $8.00 – 10.00.

Chattanooga Choo Choo.
$8.00 – 10.00. Horseshoe
Curve, Altoona, Pennsylvania. $8.00 – 10.00.

ABOVE: Underground, Atlanta — underground shopping mall. $6.00 – 8.00. Pioneer Village. $8.00 – 10.00. Santa Claus, Indiana. $10.00 – 12.00.

RIGHT: Two domes from Santa's Village — there's probably one in every state! $8.00 – 10.00 each.

Knott's Berry Farm, California. $8.00 – 10.00. Cedar Point, Ohio — an amusement park near Cleveland. $10.00 – 12.00.

Mount Rushmore, Black Hills, South Dakota. $10.00 – 12.00. Deer Forest, Coloma, Michigan. $10.00 – 12.00.

Enchanted Forest. $8.00 –10.00.
Solvang, California. $8.00 – 10.00.

Perry's Tropical Nut House, Belfast, Maine.
$15.00 – 18.00. Aquarena Springs, San
Marcos, Texas. $15.00 – 18.00.

Mississippi Belle, Iowa. $10.00 –
12.00. This is a nice one of two
elephants on a seesaw that
might have been for a zoo, but
the plaque is illegible. $10.00 –
12.00.

Alcatraz. Since this no
longer functions as a prison,
I guess it would classify as a
tourist attraction. Anyway, it
certainly is well known!
$10.00 – 12.00 each.

Tramway, Palm Springs. $8.00 – 10.00. Dutch Wonderland, Lancaster, Pennsylvania. $8.00 – 10.00.

Illinois Tollway. $10.00 – 12.00. Catalina Island. $8.00 – 10.00.

Baseball Hall of Fame and Museum, Cooperstown, New York. Unfortunately, many of the new domes have a lucite disc and a decal for the design. $4.00 – 6.00. National Fishing Hall of Fame, Wisconsin. $8.00 – 10.00.

Nags Head, North Carolina. $8.00 – 10.00. Cherokee, North Carolina. $8.00 – 10.00. Mackinac Island, Michigan. $8.00 – 10.00.

Hershey Park, Pennsylvania. $8.00 – 10.00. Statue of Liberty (probably in more domes than any other image). $8.00 – 10.00.

Disneyland, California. In December of 1992, I was in Disney World, Florida — the home of souvenirs and kitsch — and there wasn't one snow dome to be had! $20.00 – 22.00. Los Angeles County Museum. $15.00 – 20.00.

Gateway Arch. $12.00 – 15.00. The Astrodome, Houston, Texas. $12.00 – 15.00.

The Spruce Goose™ 1984 HFB Corp. Howard Hughes' monster flying boat made of birch. $12.00 – 15.00. Queen Mary, Long Beach, California. $20.00 – 22.00.

Grand Canyon National Park. $12.00 – 15.00. Pikes Peak, Colorado. $10.00 – 12.00.

Mt. Rainier, Washington. $12.00 – 15.00. Glacier National Park, Montana — this dome is new; and yet the goat is three dimensional and free standing; there is no lucite disc, and the background is not a decal. It can be done! $8.00 – 10.00.

Ausable Chasm, New York. $8.00 – 10.00. Grandfather Mountain, North Carolina. $8.00 – 10.00. Bryce Canyon — I wonder if we all refused to buy these, would they stop making them? $6.00 – 8.00.

Yellowstone Park. $8.00 – 10.00. Niagara Falls. $8.00 – 10.00. Cairns — Great Barrier Reef. $12.00 – 15.00.

Royal Gorge, Colorado. $8.00 – 10.00. Great Smoky Mountains. $8.00 – 10.00. Bear Mountain, New York (the lodge looks just like this). $12.00 – 15.00.

Stand Rock, Wisconsin Dells. $8.00 – 10.00. Grand Canyon. $10.00 – 12.00. Crater Lake. $8.00 – 10.00.

Yosemite. This is a new style — writing the name on the dome with a decal. $6.00 – 8.00. Columbia Icefield, Jasper, Canada. The glacier is a mile deep! $12.00 – 15.00.

Great Smoky Mountains. $8.00 – 10.00. Mount Rainier. $10.00 – 12.00.

Natural Bridge Caverns, Texas; Cave of the Winds; Crystal Cave, Pennsylvania. $8.00 – 10.00 each.

Luray Caverns; Meramec Caverns — hideout of Jesse James; Skyline Caverns, Virginia. $8.00 – 10.00 each.

Howe Caverns, New York; Mammoth Cave, Kentucky; Dixie Caverns, Salem, Virginia. $8.00 – 10.00 each.

Nassau; United States Virgin Islands. $10.00 – 12.00 each.

Lake Tahoe — calendar base. $10.00 – 12.00. Marineland — calendar base. $12.00 – 15.00.

Puerto Rico. $8.00 – 10.00. Niagara Falls, Canada (with the ubiquitous rainbow). $6.00 – 8.00.

Atlantic City, New Jersey — showing the now defunct Steel Pier. A tiny dome of Atlantic City, and what it's famous for. $15.00 – 20.00.

The Pier — Old Orchard Beach, Maine. $15.00 – 18.00.

Hawaii. $10.00 – 12.00.

Puerto Rico. $8.00 – 10.00. Guam, USA. $12.00 – 15.00.

My son bought these in Puerto Rico, and said they were being sold to celebrate the Anniversary of Columbus' landing; they were supposed to represent his three ships. However, these ships are rather generic and have been used in other domes. $6.00 – 8.00 each.

War between the States. $8.00 – 10.00. Cadet Chapel, West Point. $10.00 – 12.00.

Eternal Light, Gettysburg, Pennsylvania. $15.00 – 18.00. Fort Markley, Seneca, Kansas. $15.00 – 18.00.

Watkins Glen, New York. $10.00 – 12.00. Ft. Leonard Wood, Missouri. $25.00 – 28.00.

Desert Storm dome with the flag placed in the sand. $12.00 – 15.00. Ft. McHenry, Baltimore, Maryland — birthplace of the Star Spangled Banner. $12.00 – 15.00.

Rebel Country — Confederate flag and cannon. $12.00 – 15.00. Graceland with Elvis' plane flying overhead. $12.00 – 15.00.

TOP LEFT: Cooper Union, New York City — an educational institution founded by Peter Cooper in 1859. $20.00 – 22.00.

TOP RIGHT: The Guggenheim Museum, New York City, designed by Frank Lloyd Wright, and added to in 1992. These new domes, made in Germany, depict the museum with its addition. There is a day and a night version. There is no plaque, so when I ordered them, I asked for their labels to identify the boxes. $12.00 – 18.00 each.

CENTER ABOVE: Mackinac Bridge. $8.00 – 10.00. Stanford University, Palo Alto, California. $10.00 – 12.00.

CENTER BELOW: Faneuil Hall — the Cradle of Liberty, Boston, Massachusetts. $12.00 – 15.00. Lake Champlain. These were purchased in Burlington, Vermont. The ferry moves in a slot. $8.00 – 10.00.

BOTTOM: Gillette Castle, Hadlyme, Connecticut. This castle was built by William Gillette for his wife. He then left it to the state and it is now part of a state park. The oval dome is the older one. $8.00 – 10.00. The rectangular one is new; it does have the actual shape of the castle, however, without resorting to decals, and plastic discs! $6.00 – 8.00.

INDY 500. Black dome, printing on outside of base; but racing car, flags and spectators make very clear that this is not a generic dome. $10.00 – 12.00. The Alamo, San Antonio, Texas. $8.00 – 10.00.

Lake Winnipesaukee and Mount Washington, New Hampshire. $12.00 – 15.00. The Balsalms, Dixville Notch, New Hampshire. $10.00 – 12.00.

Lincoln's Home, Springfield, Illinois. $12.00 – 15.00. Betsy Ross House, Philadelphia, Pennsylvania. $12.00 – 15.00.

The United Nations Building, calendar base. $18.00 – 22.00. New York City, calendar base. $12.00 – 15.00.

Old North Church, Boston — where Paul Revere saw the lights: "One if by land, two if by sea." $6.00 – 8.00. The Dalton Gang Hideout — McCade, Kansas. $8.00 – 10.00.

Ellis Island, New York — landing place of the immigrants, and recently redone as a visitors' center and historic monument. $6.00 – 8.00. Corn Palace, Mitchell, South Dakota. $8.00 – 10.00. Witch City, Salem, Massachusetts. $6.00 – 8.00.

Hammond Castle, Gloucester, Massachusetts. $10.00 – 12.00. Hearst Castle, San Simeon, California. $12.00 – 15.00.

Two more calendar bases: L.A. Chinatown. $20.00 – 22.00. California. $8.00 – 10.00.

Martinique. When the name is painted on the outside of the base, one gets the feeling that this dome with its ever present sailboat and palm trees could be used for many different locales. $8.00 – 10.00. This globe has a distinct Caribbean flavor, and printing in the background. $10.00 – 12.00.

Florida. Couple on a seesaw, calendar base. $8.00 – 10.00. Florida — flamingo. $6.00 – 8.00.

Perdido Key, Florida (same as a Puerto Rico dome). $6.00 – 8.00. Ft. Walton Beach. $6.00 – 8.00.

Ft. Lauderdale — more flamingos. $6.00 – 8.00. Catalina Island, California. This is an older dome and more unique with the building and the flying fish. $15.00 – 18.00.

Outer Banks, North Carolina — coral and fish. $8.00 – 10.00. Cape Hatteras, North Carolina — sailboat and light house. $8.00 – 10.00. Myrtle Beach, South Carolina — surfer and sailboat. $8.00 – 10.00.

Palm Springs — giraffe and rainbow. $10.00 – 12.00. Palm Springs. Penguins, icebergs, and still the rainbow. $10.00 – 12.00.

Lake Tahoe — two sailboats on a seesaw. $8.00 – 10.00. Barbados — sailboat in a small square dome. $10.00 – 12.00.

St. Thomas, Virgin Islands, blue fish and coral. $10.00 – 12.00. Destin, Florida, three master and clouds. $6.00 – 8.00.

Cape May, New Jersey. I bought many different domes in Cape May, from different stores and at different times. In every one, the light blue paint came off the back and flaked into the water. These were all made in China, but I've had many other domes from China, and none have done this. Does anyone have any ideas? $6.00 – 8.00. St. Martin. Large dome, ocean liner, many palm trees, and no lucite! $10.00 – 12.00.

Key West — a pirate ship with three pirate children in the foreground. $8.00 – 10.00. Key West — sailor on boat. Inside dome says "I want to see the world." $6.00 – 8.00.

The same dome in a smaller size from Cape Cod; Cape Cod with a lobster and sea gull. $6.00 – 8.00 each.

Another Cape Cod; Lake George, New York. $8.00 – 10.00 each.

WORLD'S FAIRS AND COMMEMORATIVES

New York World's Fair 1964 – 65.

Moon Landing, tall dome all silver. $20.00 – 22.00. Moon Landing. Small oval dome shows lunar craft and astronauts, German made. $10.00 – 12.00.

The end of the Berlin Wall, 1989. It's amazing that such an historic and important event should end up depicted in a snow dome, but here it is. $20.00 – 25.00. The Olympic Games in Munich, 1972. $20.00 – 25.00.

Winter Olympics, Albertville, France, 1992. $12.00 – 15.00. The Vatican Pavilion at the New York World's Fair, 1964 – 1965. $20.00 – 25.00.

Seville, Spain — the Seville Expo. The Barcelona Olympic Games, 1992. Dome on right says Barcelona in background. $15.00 – 18.00 each.

ABOVE, LEFT AND RIGHT: Arizona Memorial. Contains two different fluids; the water below "sea level" is blue, above is clear. This is a large squat dome that is very rare; they were withdrawn from the market because the clear liquid often got cloudy. $45.00 – 60.00.

RIGHT: Two different versions of the New York World's Fair Unisphere dome. This first set (day and night) is the common set — very available. The quality is inferior and the background is murky. $6.00 – 8.00 each.

These domes of the same image are very scarce; the quality is far superior. Notice how distinct the buildings in the background are. $20.00 – 25.00 each.

153

Seattle World's Fair. $15.00 – 18.00 each.

Expo '74 Spokane, USA. $15.00 – 18.00. Expo '86 Vancouver, Canada. $8.00 – 12.00.

500th Anniversary of the Bahamas, 1492 – 1992. $15.00 – 20.00. 150 years of the Deutsche Eisenbahnen (Railroads) 1835 – 1985. Dortmunder Presse Ball, 1983 – a black tie affair for the press. $15.00 – 20.00.

Small dome has six people in moving boat in front of historic buildings. $12.00 – 15.00. Atomium is from the 1958 World's Fair in Brussels. $35.00 – 40.00.

ZOOS AND AQUARIUMS

Most of the new zoo and aquarium domes are rectangular plastic with a description of the animal printed on the back.

Metro Toronto Zoo — three dimensional animal. $12.00 – 15.00. Greater Los Angeles Zoo — who's looking at whom? $15.00 – 20.00.

Bronx Zoo — polar bears on ice floes. $15.00 – 20.00. Southwick Wild Animal Farm — deer and moose, nice pine trees. $15.00 – 20.00.

Two more domes from the Metro Toronto Zoo — both with nice backgrounds and three dimensional animals. $12.00 – 15.00 each.

A good looking lion from Toronto. $12.00 – 15.00.

Birmingham Zoo — it must be hard to keep a polar bear cool in Alabama. $15.00 – 18.00. St. Louis Zoo — animals are decals on a lucite background. $6.00 – 8.00. Indianapolis Zoo — same dome as the Bronx Zoo, and the plaques are on the inside. $10.00 – 12.00.

Hogle Zoo. $10.00 – 12.00. Calgary Zoo, Canada — black dome and decals. $10.00 – 12.00.

Marineland — with porpoises. $8.00 – 10.00. A nice one from Marineland in a drum. $18.00 – 20.00.

Three new domes: New York Aquarium (Coney Island). Mystic, Marinelife Aquarium, Connecticut. A slightly different dome from the same place. One has snow and the other, gold glitter. $6.00 – 8.00 each.

Sea World of Florida — this is a nice dome with its row of penguins. $8.00 – 10.00. Vancouver Aquarium, Stanley Park. $10.00 – 12.00. Marine World, Africa, USA. $8.00 – 10.00.

Marine World — a ring toss game. $6.00 – 8.00. New England Aquarium, Boston, Massachusetts. $10.00 – 12.00.

Marineland of the Pacific — nice background; three dimensional fish. $10.00 – 12.00. Marineland — featuring "Bubbles" the whale. $8.00 – 10.00.

SAVE OUR PLANET!

These four domes urge us all to save the Earth. $10.00 – 12.00 each. The captions read:
1. We must help stop the destruction of the rain forest.
2. We must help preserve our National Parks and Wilderness areas.
3. We must help protect endangered birds and their habitats.
4. We must stop polluting our oceans, and destroying the marine life (center picture).

Fourth Save the Earth dome, discussed above. Kenora — Husky says "Prevent water pollution." It's good to see that a snow dome can carry an important ecological and social message! $10.00 – 12.00.

This last dome is truly unique. David Peters received it as a gift from his wife. The top half shows a woodsman selling Christmas trees to a business man. In the lower half, the trees are gone and the woodsman has to buy artificial trees from the manufacturer. In effect, the woodsman has sold off his heritage. Save our forests! The dome is made of handblown glass and is one of a kind; the base is also glass. It was executed by Canadian artist Wendy Allen and purchased at a craft show in Baltimore. $150.00 – 200.00.

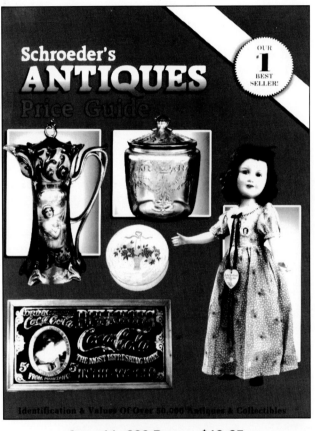